THE WORD IN EDGEWISE

THE WORD IN EDGEWISE

Poems by Sean M. Conrey

In memory of my father,
James Gant Conrey, 1943-2013

Acknowledgements

The following poems were published, often in another form, in the
following journals.

"Suburban Beirut Nocturne," *Sukoon: Art. Poetry. Prose.* volume 1,
    issue 2, Summer 2013.

"Prayer for Prometheus," *Post: A Review of Poetry Studies*, no. 2,
    Spring 2010.

"A History of Naming," *Post: A Review of Poetry Studies*, no. 2, Spring
    2010.

"Anxiety in the Garden of Weeds," *Baltimore Review*, Vol. 13, no. 2,
    Summer/Fall 2009.

"First Light," *Georgetown Review*, Vol. 10, issue 1, Spring 2009.

"The Word in Edgewise," *Notre Dame Review*, no. 27, Winter/Spring
    2009.

"Prognosis: Cataract," *Notre Dame Review*, no. 27, Winter/Spring
    2009.

"Dowry Aubade," *Tampa Review*, no. 36, Winter 2008.

"Animating the Ruin," *Hayden's Ferry Review*, no. 43, Fall/Winter
    2008-9.

"a chicago," *American Letters and Commentary*, no. 19, 2008.

"Insomniac's Aubade," *Midwest Quarterly* Vol. XLIX, no. 1, Autumn
    2007.

"Forest Ridge Farms Nocturne" *Hiram Poetry Review*, Issue 68,
    Spring 2007.

"Poem in the Light of a Black and White Television," *Midwest
    Quarterly*, Vol. XLVIII, no. 3, Summer 2006.

"To a Man on Break," *Plainsongs* Vol. XXV no. 3, Spring 2005.

"A Small Fight Involving Sheep Cheese" *Notre Dame Review*, no. 18,
    Summer 2004.

"On Diffidence" *Cream City Review* Vol. 28, no. 1, Spring 2004.

"Present Perfect Tense" featured in *Diptera, Memphis Flyer* online
    edition Feb 7, 2003-Feb 14, 2003.

"A Conversation with the Living," "A History of Naming," "Poem in the Light of a Black and White Television," "Prognosis: Cataract," and "A Prayer for Nola" appeared in the chapbook *A Conversation with the Living*, published by Finishing Line Press, November 2009.

I would like to thank the following people, all of whom played a role in helping this book along:

I am grateful to my parents, Jim and Phyllis Conrey, who trusted me. Debby Davies, my first and continuous teacher and true friend. Arnie Johnston, Bill Olsen, Nancy Eimers and Mark Halliday for their dedication and help at Western Michigan. Don Platt, Marianne Boruch, Richard Cecil, Wendy Flory, Pat Sullivan, Thomas Rickert and Janice Lauer at Purdue for their care, attention and friendship. Richard Tillinghast, Ellen Bryant Voigt and Tony Hoagland who advanced me as I retreated. The staff and editors at the *Sycamore Review*, especially Barney Haney, Neal Gill, Cody Lumpkin, and Sarah Green. The editors who put their faith in these poems. And fellow travelers, family and friends: Shannon Conrey and Dan Boron, Nada Fadda, Jason Arkles, Stephen and Bets Davies, Jamie Thomas, Mel Favara, Lesha Shaver, Barb Lawhorn-Harroun, Phil Crymble, Derek Zoeteway, Anne Zimmerman-Reich, Emily Koehn, Jessica Reed, Henry Hughes, Willard Greenwood, Rob Davidson, Laura Williams, Russ Brickey, Geof Carter and Sara JacobsCarter, Karl Stolley, Amy Ferdinandt Stolley, Julie Staggers, Murray Shugars. The *Words on the Go* crew, especially Pam Judd and Kevin McKelvey. Melanie Gee, Jenny Spinner, Jesse Nissim, Patrick Williams, Dana Olwan, Farha Ternikar, David McCallum, Brigid Dunn, and Ghassan Zeineddin. And lastly, of course, Carol and our daughters Mira and Emily who are shuffled into all these poems and who made sure they got written with love.

CONTENTS

ONE

TWO

THREE

FOUR

ONE

Animating the Ruin

Enough of this trying age of buying things:
let's knot some words into the thing dying closest,
and when the onus falls, let's shuffle the jokers
back into the deck, paint dancesteps on sidewalks
and sing the whole way, teaching tunes
that lead to bold dancing. In light of such majesty,
junkyard trumpets are raised and bellow their call:
the time has come for harmonicas. Let's walk
the interstate medians in graceless highwire decadence
till the highway's a logjam of left-behind cars,
the parking lot's full of fire pits, tents
and tambourines. Pilgrims all, let's take the reins
of black and white horses and drive well again.
By God what a racket worth hearing we'll make.

Tsunami

It starts with a long shot, the beach almost white,
the water's edge pulled far below the tide mark.
For a second or two the camera pulls in on a dot,
a man so far in the distance it's unclear it's a man,
standing in perfect posture, vertical and still
facing east, where the wave builds into a fist.
The camera's rushed to higher ground, scans
only briefly back to the shore as it tilts up stairs
intended surely for a safe escape from a fire,
now leading up to the balconies and roof where
tourists shout and point, their voices ripping.
By now the wave is clearly in view, the camera
holder says, in what must be Swedish, Look, there!
turning back, steadily holding another moment
on the dot, still standing but now leaning in a little.
The water washes him like dust on a patio away
and by then, the camera's on the move again.
Below, an old couple scrounge for a rail or ball,
a truck licks against a wall, its bed full of children,
the pool fills with mud, a woman grabs a ladder,
a boat with a family somehow in it glides by quietly.
But these we all see, and the calamity is so clear.
They died or didn't die. Some lived to say they saw
their homes, the swimming pool, the bare dirt
walkway to the shore they'd trod for days before
all sweep by. The old couple are surely dead.
The children in the truck bed, probably, too. So
why, when dwelling after, months past, now,
do I return instead to the indistinguishable dot
who walked out only when the earthquake settled
and the water receded and the warnings blared?
While others wildly sought stairs and rooftops

and hillside gardens to clamber to, he instead said,
"Enough, already. A will greater than my own to live
has made my life a gift and gives me a choice."
How rare a soul with foresight enough to share
that with us, we who, as he stood staring calmly,
scrambled away in a fury and were left strangely
behind in his wake, reminded of what? Water?

We Wait Patiently

The light breaking through
the tough black rolls of clouds,
so firm and fat with rain,
marks the sky behind them
like a bruise, a bruise like God gives
when He paddles the world's ass.

And the ark in the distance
tilts to one side
as elephants stand, watching
the ocean lift
a humid white to the horizon
where the sun rises, red.

And an olive's topmost branch
finally bends in the wind
till the dove breaks it,
flies across the crest
to everyone standing on deck—

Not waiting, really,
rather watching the sunrise fiercely,
the first in forty days,
as yet without our bearings.

A Prayer for Nola

Lord, the river's feet tripped till
it filled the streets with trembling,
then soft, hot silence for days—

if we could see, really see,
your calm and quiet, these gnats
drifting on the river's long neck—

if we could see the river without us,
all solitude without loneliness,
we'd learn the first of all joys—

a chalk-handed nun whispers
for us to hear it, too. Listen and stare,
she says, learn the good fear—

it brings us into our skin, alone
and ready for love in spite of it all.

On Scripture, Water and the Vegetal Realm

I've found reasons to distrust reason's
power to cull meaning from lilies
that clutch at the soil for days
before breaking through. The overlay
of a few facts and geometry's thin
vacancies hint an outline, mint copies
on the page but fail to fill in the gaps.

~*~

Consider a waterfall's pool moving
(clearly it's so: the oak leaves drift),
and in this evident slowness we point,
saying what we see, naively believing
words and things are fully requited,
never virgins, the knots in the text
twisted through water, leaf and word,
bowline perfect, however they're said
they're always and still making love.

~*~

Consider how easily we overwrite:
The trees on shore bend black in the wind,
the river's sewer breaks a waft across
in a thin ripple trilling the trees and then
the voice of a small white sail catching.
This is all in the wind? We may say so,
but the breeze falls like a pheasant:
a seven-man firing squad's had its way.

~*~

Hold the botany book near the lily,
the lens flares as we focus from one
to the other: the page, a petal, the page,
the stamen, the page that digresses
at length on the anther and others
that detail the style and the stigma
and by then we've lost the poor flower
before us in favor of the scripture.

                ~*~

Sound advice would be: don't mistake
a finger for the flower it points to.
And are words fingers or the memory
strings tied round fingers? Maybe
they're lassos that span the otherwise
cold distance from hands to flowers?
Does folding our hands in prayer
weave their weft in the lily's warp?

                ~*~

How many eyes does the page absorb
in church, men in stained-glass light
looking at the dance of black and white
like teenagers texting at Niagara Falls.
Magnificent bastard, I read your book!
Why in hell would we choose to be
born again between the white thighs
of some book when, if we just look up,
what we've read is busy being born?

Anxiety in the Garden of Weeds

Where underneath the plastic sheets
        there winds a root around a rock;
where over the rise the creek bend silts
        and builds the waterworn weeds in silence;
where some thread tugs my ear to listen
        to the wind's news of my children asleep;
where love nets me from setting adrift,
        though I'm alone in a city of millions;
when starting, a bird lifts its wings on a wire
        and settles closer to the glass bell;
when bracing for the water's cold,
        so too the step forward, so too the wince;
when chalklines snap to gauge how lines
        can make the bent world seem bearable;
where snow films black and shivers in
        to whet some stone's edge again;
where in the weeds trodden long before snow
        the snapped stick says the hunt was on;
when in the meltwater a mineral stirring
        warms and cues a clutch of seeds to split;
when topside the sun draws a thistle
        on its course, a child watching her parent;
where women share a common match
        with the moon's reliable candle;
where bricklayers and stonemasons pave
        roads woven in stone, threaded with mud;
when the tea of a saltmarsh pours light
        and calm through reeds bent and broken;
what time is made of when furious children
        throw bikes and books over bridges;
what a distance that shadow made
        when we stood cold that day, remember;

where the hollow wrap of a blanket
        riddled with leaves sits rotting riverside;
what the lake was like before the storm,
        before lightning struck its far edge;
how many berries round the tree fell
        and blew this way against odds;
where the oak canopy caps its dark over
        and irons a smudge of mud this long;
how often that cold wave crested
        before some boat came by to part it;
where we walk right past the sidewalk's
        old concrete hands without seeing;
when I made like I was gauging the sun,
        held my thumb up to dampen its cornice;
when waking, the rattle from yesterday
        comes back and clamors all the more;
where glass shattered in view of heaven
        and fell, setting us back some years;
what light this is some mornings waking
        and god I cannot see it, or my part.

Big Creek

The stone, still
in the water,
after many years
moored mostly
to itself, but still
thankfully there,
writes the rill
so it fills a deep
hole and scoops
the bank, darkly
marking a place
fully out of reach
from the dock
where we sit
saying so little
and stone still.

A History of Naming

Maybe the words drew across the plains
like wind through wheat,
touched cold lakes thick with pollen
and heavy fog, flew past woodpiles,
past the chipped brick sides
of tall red homes sitting stoic
in the Midwest, then finally became
breath and foundered at the end

of a pen, driven out
through the body like sap in a cedar,
or a stop sign near the tracks,
out of necessity and safety,
words like houses, carved out
of the woods nearby into rows,
cut like granite or marble,
piled and shaped into spaces
big enough to inspire a silence
a playground full of children
couldn't fill, not even if
they all had garden hoses,
not even if the words were like

water itself, the nearly inaudible sound
of the river rubbing shore,
barges, brigantines and schooners,
docked on quays with stringlights
and piss streams and champagne
bottles broken on a sloop's bow,
as rose petals drift in the flotsam
from a torrent that struck upstream

at midnight, till the bodies bring
newsmen, flashbulbs and headlines
printed in ink by the gallon,
newsprint used for paper boats
set aflame and set afloat

in fire and smoke, words founded
the day we began, in lightning perhaps,
or a brushfire, words now tied to
tongues of flame deep in the boiler,
or the uranium atom controlled,
the unseen fire that kills without pause,
and then so many words for death.

Should Your Time Be Meted Today

In a red boat, he's fishing, alone,
so you wave till he groans a bit, points
to the bobber and signs one minute.
Which passes, so he packs it in. Bait
drags the surface as he rows for you.

What do you say to the ferryman
when you arrive with no bribe? No
full flask, or pennies on your eyes.
It's a sunken feeling, like living, really,
though you're nearly on the other side.

Says his name's Elias, fishes here
most days, when he works at all.
Otherwise, he stays with his wife,
who never sleeps at home, and so
her silence and eyes send him off.

Doing well, before you kicked it?
he asks. I'd gotten stranger-friendliness
down, you say, but still barked
too often at the wife. Gave some
to charity, but skimped on family time.

At least you're not a liar, he sighs.
At least you own up, after the fact.
Better'n I ever did. They took
pity on me, gave me eternity to work
it out, fishing. Took years, but

I've come to know there's no fish
in this river. Most mornings the mist

spoons me like it's holding me
in its palm, though. About as touched
as I ever feel. That said, I'll take you.

That's it? No Peter, no trumpet, no
clouds? Nope, none, he says. Chiggers
and cattails at the river's edge's the best
you can do these days. Though I hear
the fishing's better on the other side.

The World Tent

Its thick denim's sagged low overnight.
Its wet cast weighs on me, waking.
The sun slowly steams the fog
till I slither out and step to work.

First I lift the poles beneath.
The ground seeps brown at my feet.
I place the stakes and hammer:
the sledge's weight does all the work.

My father always said it would.
'In soft ground, run them deep,'
he says, and also 'Lash them taut
so the rain drains off it better.'

But there's a runner in the weft.
Threads spin and tear at the edge
as I hook the guides again and again.
When it's vaulted high, I take a rest.

In the rough-spun shade I watch it fray
in hope the heft will hold all day.

If It's a Riverview You Seek

Spoil yourself for a time in quiet
where the tall grass folds up under,
and look long across the river
with nothing asunder but this

thistle twig poking, which ruins
the scene as you stare to a cove
where the hot sun's striking
lines of light on the water's edge—

just because the tall grass grates,
the light dividing water from wood
somehow makes it seem, we fools,
these things and us are separate.

Autumn

We'd rather it's not true
that you are winter's door
unless the door is open
and also summer's.

We'd rather the wind
blowing through both
blew back and forth,
though we only think on it

when kites and leaves,
cold-slowed bees
and low-slung clouds
pour out the door

one way. Bracing ourselves,
one hand holds the jamb,
the other an umbrella
that catches and pulls

till the rug at our feet
gathers, chairs and shoes
pile up at the threshold.
Oh, have it your way.

If Fate Be Real, Let's Set About To Praise It

There's the wheel, and by the "wheel" I mean the day
when the spoke comes round, not the whole thing,
just the point when I notice it spinning. The way
it comes on like a children's choir when a girl sings

too soon and the rest of the room moves to shape
itself around her and then everyone claps, smiling
at the mishap. Except, when the wheel turns, I break
a bit, and the months that follow are spent idling.

The clouds pound their way horizontal, a match
lights a white candle when the sun's last shadow's
past. By past I mean out of now like a door latch
flipped a dozen times by a man decluttering

his head through repetition. By repetition is meant
how the footman comes up and needs kicking,
or the streetworn harp player who bends into
his sorrow, whose days begin and end with shouting.

And on and on, my lungs crutched on by a pill
I've taken, and the shallow breaths are thrilling,
since by breath I mean life and by life is meant still
here, and here is the work I do to make a living.

But there's a voice beyond the bend of the wheel
that says something new, to which I mean
overbearing, and it stammers beyond the windowsill
gently muttering to itself and quietly swearing

to god. By god I mean the hand on the wheel.
And it says 'Let's dance by a fire in the clearing

at midnight.' I say I can't, I'll be sleeping, I'll
be dreaming of knots, I keep an ongoing

record of weaver's eights and bowlines, yarns
fill my head till the sun slips in and brings
it to an end. But just before, a few scattered stars.
By stars I mean strangers, quietly weaving.

TWO

A Conversation with the Living

1. Believing the Age of Miracles To Be Over

After Saint Francis swam,
it's said the water tasted like honey.
Funny I'd feel him here
behind the pumphouse of my apartment,
whispering to please note the beetles
in the bright holes of sunshine at my feet.

Francis, can I borrow some time with you
my grandmother would've used,
if she'd been given a chance?
Dead at forty-five. But you knew that.
I'm sure you've been kept abreast
of the animal tragedies since your own.

Tell me, is God like a big hole,
or a bright light? Do all the stars fall at once?
The sea glass over under His windy hand?

Here, on the new edge of town,
I'm thinking of you, your flat world and its edge,
all that gold leaf and stone in the woods,
you humming counterpoint to birdsong,
a big leaf used as an umbrella.

As a boy I had faith and always felt
you'd come down some night
on a donkey almost cartoon-like,
and we'd ride to the playground,

walk the wrong way up the slide

and just keep walking, each cloud
a step higher. It's so simple,
isn't it? Nice. Something you'd like.
It ain't quite Blake, I admit, who
saw angels pour white and blue light
through a burr oak as a child.

I once read that a man in Texas saw Mary
grace a lake's surface south of Dallas
(like a bomb, but beautiful, he said).
The same night a Detroit jeweler caught
an angel circling the moon as it eclipsed.
Lying by his pool, the AC humming,
it shook its hair and the sky fell around him.
He missed work for a week and didn't speak
even to his wife who was luckily patient.

Near Spokane, the river ran red,
a woman said, though she'd been drinking,
and not a soul for miles around
believed her. North of here,
on Lake Superior, people every year
watch lights spin across the lake like milk
down a sink.

The real ones: the aurora, ball lightning,
maybe snowblindness or mirage. I'm afraid

I'm rambling. I'll cut to the chase.
Please, tomorrow, when the sun comes up,
help my father pull through, if you can.
He's fifty-seven, twelve years past
where his mother ever was.
On the dash of my car is the letter

he gave me if something goes wrong.
But you already knew that.

2. Driving There

In the morning I woke in the dark.
The smooth walls, the scientific smell
of the air conditioner,
the salt and dust taste of waking.
How it all looks from the outside,
everyone driving to church
past my sliding door lit in an arc of yellow.

I fried eggs and called my mother,
already dressed across town.
Already hot, the deep weeds
held tight around the step stones
leading to the lot. I drove over.
She waited on the porch swing,
her jacket zipped to the top,
her feet an inch off the ground.
I unlocked the door, said good morning.

Morning, she said, brushed off the seat,
and sat. Nearly a week since I'd seen her.
He'll be under from eight to noon,
she said, glancing to where the horizon
barely lit above the chain link fence,
where the neighbors' yards spread out
in neat angles of mums and tomatoes.

Your sister can't make it, she said,
opened and shut the glove box,
the light too bright on her make-up.
He'll understand. At least he'll claim to.
She nodded out the passengerside.
The highway empty, the road signs

for cigarettes and hairspray underlit
like coming attractions.

Your father misses you, she said.
Sometimes the crossword's tough,
and he says he knows you'd know.

The buildings downtown
came through the trees like a staircase
to nowhere in particular.

The surgeon gave me a pass,
we can park for free, she said.
Just hang it on the rearview,
the man should let us through.

Waiting room, seventh floor,
the nurse pointed to the elevator door.
A cold wind blew from a vent.
A plastic plant draped down a planter.

The door opened and we rode up.
Between the third and fourth floor
I looked at her for the first time.
She smiled kind of, blinked and looked up
to where the numbers click by.

3. Lunchbreak

Alone while everyone else got lunch,
the closest thing to silence was the IV
dripping. His toes kept coming uncovered.

You ask out that girl from work yet, son?
No. I don't think she's the one, Pop.
She doesn't have to be to date her.
His breath was short under the noseclip.
Your mother was nineteen when I met her.
I know, Pop, I said and flipped my magazine.
I was working the door at this jazz joint,
and I let her in. I let her in.

The sun hung brown in the tinted window.
Put that magazine down a second, son.
You ever thought about me dying?
You're not gonna die, Pop. Some day I will,
he said. Well, sure, yeah.

I wrote your grandfather a letter
when he died, then I burned it. Seems pagan,
doesn't it? Seems natural to me, I said.
He closed his eyes and breathed deep.
A nurse came in, checked the drip and left.

Did you go to church Sunday? No.
Will your sister be in today? Probably later,
if at all. She's a hard worker, that one.
I remember that cheesecake

in that girl scout contest, he said. You remember?
I remember she came in second, I said.
Was it second? Yes.

You like that job your mother got you?
It's better than nothing.
You stay at it and they'll move you up.
That's what they say.

You written anything for the paper lately?
No.
Your mother loves when you do.
I know.

I always wanted to write, you know that?
Yeah, I know.
Your grandmother was quite the poet.
So you've said.
The apple doesn't fall too far—

I'm gonna go grab a cup of coffee, Pop,
you need anything?
No.

4. Late Night Phone Call from My Sister

There was one tree
out my bedroom window
backlit by a floodlight.
With the screen pulled,
the fountain in the lake
sounded like a dead channel.
And the phone rang.

It's me. How is he?
Well, they say he'll be okay.
Was he conscious?
He asked about you.
But the surgery was alright?
They gave him too much morphine,
his heart was ten beats a minute.

In the kitchen I opened
the microwave for light.

He said he wants to see you, I said.
When are they letting him out?
Thursday, sometime.
Afternoon or morning?
Not sure. Thursday.

The milk was spoiled.
I boiled water for coffee.
She sounded like those old women
on break at the factory.
I could hear her smoking.

He gave me a letter

in case something goes wrong, I said.
Did you read it?
Nothing's gone wrong.

You still leaving Friday? she asked.
If all goes well from now to then.
It'll be good for you to get away.
I'm afraid I'll go crazy if I stay.

Jumbled siren dots of an ambulance
flew past on the highway.

You said he asked about me? she said.
I told him you had to work.
You did, didn't you?
Yes.
Good. I try not to lie in hospitals.

5. Before Work

This is how someone gives in to drowning,
or slips away slowly in a snowstorm.
I woke to the woman next door making love,
the man upstairs pacing his kitchen with his coffee.
I closed my eyes and breathed in her liquid,
the sound of her, the stale smell of my bedsheets.
Michael, she kept saying. The back of my mind
rubbed raw. Light broke through the blinds

in hot bars. Michael. Is it 7:03 AM?
Michael, take me. I hung my feet off the bed.
Yes, darling, he answered, old fashioned. Yes.
I stood in a pile of clothes on the floor.
Michael. Take her far from here, she needs it.
Michael. The archangel come back to the suburbs.
Michael. Admit it's hard to be a man.
Michael. Yes, darling, I'm here. I'm here.
I slipped off my shorts in the bathroom. There!

There! The shower was only lukewarm
this time of morning. The soap
smelled like opium. I'll go into work,
do a few things. The morning light
pushed through the sanded window.
The woman next door was quiet.
My old man was hard at work across town,
sleeping off his stitches. I closed my eyes—

him pulling me from a lake at six,
his long arm reaching out for my shirt,
the cold flash of cattails and reeds,
the bright scrape up my leg from a nail,

my father out of breath with mud on his shoes.
That could have been the end of you,
he says, and holds me up like a trophy
near the water's edge in the sunlight—

I washed my face with a soap-stiff rag,
turned off the water, got out and dried off.
I put on my pants from three days ago,
took the bank slips out of my pocket,
brushed my hair, my teeth, the lint off my shirt.
The man upstairs left down the stairwell.
Next door the woman got into her shower.

My father said he drank a fifth of whiskey
when we all went to bed that night. Alone,
on the back porch, where he'd always sit
and think about things with the light off.

6. The Story of the Tiger Lilies

When I stopped in later he was awake.
The nurse had left the bathroom light on.
Television's one bad ride, he said,
and turned it off overhead.

Looking at the ceiling he asked, opiated,
you ever been to the edge of a cliff?
Once, at Canyon DeChelly.
Cliffside ruins and a green strip
where the river runs sometimes.

No, I mean figuratively.
Like a moment of clarity?
Well, in AA's language, I guess.

When I was a kid there was a time
we went to a wedding at night,
the church lit in gold; all the lights
outside shined through the stained glass.
The priest's robes sounded like a sailboat
yawing, candlelight in his glasses,
the old smell of incense, stiff backs
as people straightened and twitched
in their brown clothes, sweating.
It all came down on me at once.
I tugged Mom's sleeve and said
I have to go to the bathroom.
So she took me. In the lobby I said,
crying, I'd forgotten where I was.
That's the best I could describe it
at eight. I guess that's less clarity

than an utter lack of vision.

I fiddled with my glasses.
Is that what you meant? Kind of.
I was thinking this morning
about my mother when I was a kid.
Course she was young, then, barely forty,
if that, and we lived on the farm
on Lily Lane. Maybe the street
makes me remember. Anyway,

playing in the house with Uncle Frank
one day, and down on the road
a gang was knocking back the weeds.
In the kitchen, my mother,
we'll say she was making peach pies,
but she could've been doing anything,
and the men caught her ear
and out she ran down the drive
to stand there while they passed,
making sure they didn't knock back
her tiger lilies. I always think of her
with her back to us, hands on hips,
seeing to it. That was all before.

I don't think I've ever mentioned it,
he said and looked over at me, quiet.

7. Journal: Prayer to No One in Particular

This afternoon I held his spoon.
The morphine made it tough to keep anything down.

Tonight the movie I rented is half-watched.
I'll leave in the morning. A week-long trip.
I'll drink a six-pack to help me sleep.

In the dark I turn off the bluescreen,
turn back the bedsheet, say to no one,
here I am, if you'll have me.
The clothes on the floor smell like yesterday
as I pull off my shirt and rub my arm.
The static of a car passes the storm window.
I write, What's the answer to the lightning rod?
The question begged by the cold air months from now?
The spiderweb in the corner?

I wonder, What is the answer between
the nail and the wood? The sweat and the skin?
The open door and the hallway?
I'd ask my father,
but he has his own trouble.
I'd ask my mother,
but she's endlessly worried.
I'd ask my sister,
but she'd say to figure it out myself.

I ask *please* to the air sitting in the sink,
the electric hum behind the fridge.
Please to my glasses blurred on the nightstand,
the sugar ring from a bottle of coke.
Please to the linseed oil rubbed into the table wood,

the steam rising round me in the shower,
the screen through the broken slat in the blinds.

I ask you this, all of you.
The thorns are filling in,
the plants push roots against the terracotta,
the carpet's frayed at the edge near the door.
Please, the earth is ripe with fruit.
I'm asking for a basket, a milkcrate, an empty bottle.
Please, my father is full of someone else's blood.

8. Alone in the Rain

I don't dream that night. But I wake
to sunlight so thick it seems the sheets are searing.
The electricity shut off in the night,
so I don't know the time. There'd been a storm.
A pile of bills on the table, next to the apples,
the keys next to them. I put the dishes
in the washer and leave them. Still early,
I cut out in the anxious quiet of the room still dead
of electricity. The air outside
heavy with drying rain and pine needles.
I put my bags in the trunk and pull away.

Nearly out of Indiana, the radio fizzles
and it gets quiet, except the window
won't go all the way up. In the hum,
the road peels back in the mirrored end
of a tanker truck. Cincinnati spills around
its glacial hills and over the Ohio.
I pull off in Newport. That quiet slip
when the world tightens around you, finally.
I take a left turn near Bellevue.
Wildflowers push against mailboxes,
my father's letter still on the dash.

Finally home, he's making his way
to his living room chair.
The sun's ninety-two million miles away
behind a cloud. My mother's alone
in the kitchen while he sleeps.
A light drizzle starts, so I hit the wipers.
A boy sits alone getting soaked in a t-shirt
on the back of a brokedown pickup.

My mother switches on the stove light.
Low clouds hang below the ones raining.
A bathtub in a pasture, cows under a low tree.
Outside of Flatwoods, I pick up
an AM dial preacher full of sermon—

Prayer's the divining rod between you and God,
he says. Hold your hands together
and the Holy Spirit will fill you up—
At sixty, the telephone poles are built music,
the corn thin and short in places,
washed out earlier in the season.
Just keep your eye on the road—
You are a thermometer, rising with the heat
of the Lord. Can you feel it? Yes—
The red of my cigarette in the windshield.
My mother pours cold water into a pot—
Now when you feel the Holy Spirit
it'll well up inside you like water behind a dam,
like a fire truck approaching. Feel it? Yes—
Rain so thick I can't see, so I pull
into a motel lot with a no vacancy sign
and naked children playing in the rain.
My mother turns the stove past high to light it—
Now hold your hands high, that's it—
My father asks for water so she gets it.
The children run inside, and I turn off the car—
God loves for you to stand tall and strong.
Make way for Jesus, he's coming back.
Make way for the Holy Spirit, it's deep inside—
Rain falls in waves through branches overhead—
The air in this church is alive—
My mother leans where the water boils—
Make way, the love that surrounds us is pure—

My father falls into a pill sleep,
and I sit waiting it out—
All aquiver with the love of mercy,
you're all saved here and now. Can you feel it?
Yes—

9. The View from Here

I grabbed the wheel with both hands.
Something sounded terrible in the quiet.
My mind had gone to seed.
I thought: A farmer burns his fields,
turns them under in the fall.
A man once shot a cannon cross a lake
to make it rain. After the great quake,
The Old Man ran backwards for a week.

But this was West Virginia.
I stopped for coffee.
The saccharine smell of the gas station.
The cashier didn't blink.
Payphone's disconnected.
Some shitbag come and cut it,
he said, and sure enough.
Stale rain dried round a soaked bag.
I took a sip, headed out.

Once it rained these little fish,
Pawpaw once told me.
His mother took it for a sign.
If the lines of the palm tell a story,
the veins beneath are a map.
Spillways round the mills in Gary.
The brick bat fields of Detroit.
A tumble-down roller rink,
weeds pouring over the eaves.
I took a good long sip.

I began to shake a bit.
It was wet and hot in the car,

white blood cells and lymph.
To either side, the trees lost their rhythm.
Their leaves fell like it was fall.
The rush of air through the window
like laundry on a too-windy day.
I blinked five seconds at a time,
the sunlight filled me with red shapes.

My old man by himself with an IV.
Small yellow flowers low in a ditch.
A man could lay in a stream and wash away.
Six miles up, a mail plane full of letters.
Mother home for her lunchbreak,
sitting silent in the kitchen with him.
A woman walks slowly across Kansas.
From orbit the constellations of cities.
The random sex of flowers taking seed.
The clumsy love of two college freshmen.
Me full of the words of the world,
spilling them.

THREE

Present Perfect Tense

This then is where we begin, Leviathan,
take the shape of a democratic vehicle –
no no no Hobbes, I deny the head of,
I mean the Commander in Chief of,
these verdant splendid fields ever-rolling
betwixt me and the next moment
(spread across the waist, the midwest,
the wide broad plain) where I find another
moment and another like those previous
in a thin cut of valley where most of us
break up the endless boredom of wartime
with the television, idle in its lights
through front windows on porches lit,
sometimes with snow or leaves unraked,
leaving me here looking vigorously,
more anxious than I'd like, trying to find
the perfect present I'm convinced
I can arrive at, even if it means forgoing
the things that clog the mind's arteries
with clutter, I mean, that clog this here
present heartily with utter loss and despair.

'Why do we all not speak to each other
at times like this, I mean, here and now?'
is a question I have asked many people
and got shrugs like a kid asked whodunit.
Maybe it's naïve to believe anyone'd answer
'No one ever talks to me and I'm lonely.'
Who'd hang their ass in that breeze,
who's willing to be that kind of vulnerable,
like meat to the cleaver or snow to the feet?
Most of us can't bear such things. Besides,

who are we to ask anything of anyone anyway?

We are people, all people, a strange thing
in this world, I might suggest, if the timing
were right and the moment didn't pass
like it can when trucks pass or the dead pass,
quickly and surely out of now forever,
reminding us that what the dead say is,
'Don't be afraid, the world is enough,'
and 'when you find a good person,
hold them like right now might go away
sometime soon' and also 'try to be nice
to the girl at the grocery store who bags.'

Though we typically like to *have* much
better than to *be,* let's see the neighbor's
porch light as the invitation it is and, six-pack
in hand, stop by for a game of cards,
and out back tell them, 'Your tomatoes
are better than ours, but we'll give you a few
of ours anyway.' Would that we came together.

Could it be it is more in the way that we,
although occasionally satisfied, rarely see
past the chainlink fence to the garden beyond,
over the goldenrod to the other side where
a bathtub is buried and painted dark blue,
made into a pond with a statuette with a hose
that pours out water solemnly, that trickles
and makes the back porch nighttime air
all the more radiant even though it isn't
exactly Buckingham Fountain, even though
we are pleased by something so small,
even though we all know that we are at war

and that people are dying or will die or
have died, that we are doing all of this —
that we could stop it maybe if we tried —

and then we could come pleasantly out
of our houses, shake hands and say,
'Hello, I've wondered where you've been
all my life, this is my wife and she likes
to cook and we'd like to have you over
and we'd like to turn off the television
and just talk,' and then years later,
having invited all our neighbors, even
the ones with the mean dog, we invite
the whole world and the whole world
comes with a passing dish and we all sit
and aren't nearly so alone, aren't so
nearly alone, nearly so much alone
here now.

Poem in the Light
of a Black and White Television

It's October so I write that this cold woman stands
arms out to me in front of a paper birch, shivering without
      a coat.

I saw the birch while listening to the news
of the war, driving my route alone tonight,

inserted her just now. She motions and there's a sound
she makes that someone else used to make.

I scribble that out and instead place her next to me in bed
with snow and morning just about to break.

But I admit the facts:

I twisted the bedsheets alone before noon today,
my clothes swallowed me before breakfast, and later,

on the ten o'clock break between crosstown deliveries,
with the room smelling like coffee and wool,

I fell asleep and dreamt I fell in love

with a Navajo girl, rode around the reservation with her
on the handlebars in the skittery, dead silence of a home
      movie.

And it ended just as I was about to wake—

with an ozone snap of celluloid and a stark white flash

through a haze of dust and smoke—

And I sat up, late evening, and it was snowing,
the cold inertia of the television dancing behind me.

Outside, the shaved fields that frame this city are miles
        away,

the red lights of radio towers barely visible through the
        trees.
I admit, there's not much to say about loneliness

when a war's just begun.

Weren't we all born at the beginning of an end, anyway?
I mean, it could be November,

the next thousand years hanging on a thread.

A Prayer for Prometheus

Prometheus, can you please light
these not yet ode-worthy things
with at least spray-painted flames

like those on gas tanks of large
black Harleys that sound at night
like monster locusts raging?

It's in good faith I ask. You see,
earlier, the machinery turned
as I walked down Orchid Street.

All the weeds pushing against
the sidewalks licked the sunlight
straight from the air, and I felt

you there, doling out the light.
Was it you who put the lanterns
in my eyes and spread the page

before me? You who stirs
embers in a censer making figures
pour from mathematicians' pens?

You who put the punk to the fuse
of the world so that I,
candle to candle, mind to mind,

would end up staring, startled
for words? If so, Prometheus,
I must say I'm finding all this fire

confusing. Could you instead
turn your torch on one thing at a time
so I could ease up to all this beauty?

Insomniac's Aubade

Some nights, I go sleepless the old way
and think dumb thoughts mostly.
Uselessly, I knead them in my head

and bake them into loaves all night
and then, come morning, come to
gently with tiny bells and write down

the thing crafted thus aslumber.
It's a failure of a way to work.
Most times, shamefully, I lose it—

the aviary keeper looses his gaggle
of birds from their cage and they
pour out my window and signal

the dawn in a flourish of sunlight
unburdened. The light spills over me
in waves and cleans me white

as an old bone. But yesterday,
just before waking, this thought came:
Have you walked outside, lately?

And I woke on the roof, unawares,
staring straight at the sun. It was
so hot already the shingles burned.

It was as if the world's strong hand
had grabbed me and handshook me

like a man who just got a job.

I sat for a bit, collected myself.
Across the alley, birds perched
on power lines, lined up like words

down a line. So I plucked them off
and plopped them down on this page
just now 'cause I think I'm supposed to.

Is that what you were saying
with all of that light? Or is this
just another one I didn't get right?

Ask What Has Fallen

how's the wife, you said she left, but still how is she.
less the movement of the tree branch, more the wind.

ask why make the bed if you're alone come nightfall.
the slight turn of the sheet points to the nightstand.

come here, I say, light out across the morning with us.
the stevedores unload bottles of sunlight on third shift.

look, three skiffs bring a welt down the sea's back.
throughway headlights push through the grey fade.

ask what's the shade writ on the back of that wall.
and what of the attic, its bare bulb from the street.

have you made your way up to the rafters, lately.
or straddled the cusp of the roof, back arched & elbows.

ask how it's all come to this, somehow, brother.
ask what's fallen on you since last you saw the stars.

To a Man on Break

Smoking a cigarette
on the ten-thirty break
he talks about the wife
of thirty years

Never laid a hand on her
Never laid a hand
on her. Never
laid a hand on her.

He takes a long drag
and stares into his
coffee. Used to
be they left a man

alone.
He punches back in
and gets to work.
Never laid a hand on her.

Poem on a Tuesday Afternoon

The punched wall
at head height,
the windfall of dust

in a noon beam.
Silence follows
and seven years

of his same sorrow
settle in again.
She knows it well.

What's not said's
a pulled tooth
a tongue runs across

until healed. On the tips
of their tongues,
she wants to absolve

him. He stares
at his knuckle, beaten red,
at the wall beside

her head and then
back at her
again. And again.

Palimpsest

Standing stained glass windows like dominos,
staring through the clutter till anthologies appear,
and here's one and there another and here's
Paul in a blue shirt, and there's Bill
on the porch, his guitar, all he owned
except a pile of petty debts, so he never said sorry
and left, last I heard, for somewhere out west.

Here's a tree in the eave, there's a shutter,
and Tracy who jerked chicken and shared
though he had nearly nothing.
A thin season for everyone, but still
we kept the lease and took the band seriously.

And what piles of beautiful debris washed up
when the weather turned cold and the snow sent
Flo back into his brokedown Buick
after his house burned, fired from McDonald's
for not having clean clothes, and he didn't see
his kids for months, his wife'd had enough,
till he worked it out, and I hope still is
all these years later 'cause I always liked Flo.

Here's a gold-painted record and a bike chain
and there's Jello Ed who'd stop by often
but never stayed longer than the liquor lasted,
and he'd talk about videos of people breaking
arms on skateboards and then leave again
for a long walk of empty lots and weeds.

So what if he never made a goddamned thing
of himself? Who am I to say it

should be otherwise? I was there too,
cigarettes falling into me like logs down a flume,
and there were still seven days in a week,
we'd fall into Sunday like a hammer
on a thumb and wait until it passed.

Here's the burnt calendar, there an ashtray
and Chili all meth-eyed, silent, sat
in his closed-off room eight hours.
And Steve lipping along to Gram Parsons
so he'd know we'd heard the real thing.
And Josh cried in his forty about this son
he didn't know, and Tom's summer spent
getting over someone who left to be happy,
and all those nights spent squinting
on the porch after dark we'd sit quiet
'cause Luke liked it quiet and so we were.

Here's a broken cassette, there's John's dog
and Julie saying he said she was the best he'd ever had,
and that made getting over him easier.
And Dan was going to be a grade school principal
and is now, and Bowser's doing pullups
in the chipped paint doorjamb of the kitchen
while the light from the stove falls out the window
and kindles the snow on the Buick.

Here's a lit candle, there's a fist through the wall,
a nightlight's white-cast pushes a shadow,
and though I sat down just now and laid it out
and though I can't really get it right, I still said it,
and so now you know, or at least you trust I do.

A Chicago

blown a glitter wind   basement sitting
bourbon st. head   long stockholm summer
then southside chicago   that one never left

hey sailor   how'd'you find the ladies room
kind of makeshift   & fabulously tightnecked
my thirteen buttons done up   righty-o ensign
if mr. mason asks   don't you tell him
then shipcall monday   stuck round after
a train to norfolk   rivets across the aftdeck

the new jersey sat days off beirut then
so we threw a new cardgame every night when

anchor hit bottom   the topside cigarette
lift the lever   remove the safety latch hatcher
no liberty there   smeared shipgrey
cross my cheeks   & she was the first said
love   redlit gal always stood still
lighting matches nights   one at a time

some other woodfloored hotel room copenhagen
shuddered to think what came of her

back stateside   years later the southside
two ace's wednesdays   tell the one bout
then snow street cabfare   smokestack hammond
frozen highgrass lake   house & storage tank

she asks where to work if not here &
a guy says why not see the world sister?

A Midwest

midfield ditches, spread welts in rows,
    fill culverts & frozen shelf ice

a small white dusting, friday afternoon girl
    finds a cigarette & walks out fieldwise

a slow fade dusk settles, marquee birds
    nestle black on white over there

mass held saturdays, st. vincent's, the boy says,
    stands, walks sixty yards out & away

chain fence thoroughfare, steel pole trafficlight,
    wool coat waiting room job

check the blindspot, frank, listen right & left,
    the hum of car slush middling

there across the parking lot, smoke it, don't bogart it,
    francis, & turn that shit up

that guy come over my place last weekend
    boozed & wanting & loud-like

come sunday afternoon that son-making absent
    father'll have his way again

I just know it's good the river ain't run over the rim,
    the creek and ditches are full

twig-dead tomato plants rattle the siding
    in the mercuryglow all night

dave's holed up in frank's basement
          three weeks back ever since he got out

every driveway sanded w/ snow & marquees
          of birds & all coming attractions

The Parable of Seeds

You see that, son,
the tree's lively circle:
the keys fall thick,

rain brings a root
till twigs twist out
and up to a new

seed that's made
to spit far as it can
in the wind, though

'far as it can' is still
in the parent's shadow.
Look, son, and see

that this new tree
that grows so well,
so close at hand

is a common kind
of child who tries
but fails to leave

the fold and so family
grows thankfully
out from that failure.

Very Short Stories

The faster-growing grass between the spigot and the
    tomatoes.

A single crushed-out butt on the mountaintop.

The blood smudge near the planter's bent nail.

The last snow in the laundry's north shadow.

A tangle of kite string on the bumper of the pickup.

The father saying, "You remember what happened last time
    you did that?"

The slight red dent where his wedding ring had been.

Three white cat skulls in the corner of the warehouse.

A solstice line of faded book spines through a broken blind.

The frost chart torn from the brittle almanac.

Old Charlie's missing trigger finger.

The weed circle where the pool used to be.

The jar of old teeth when we cleaned out her house.

The New Testament's well-thumbed edge striping the
    prison Bible.

The holes in the mall's lot where the carnival staked its tent.

A shard of windshield taped to a crutch.

Spent roman candles jammed in the treehouse roof.

The barber shop's doorstop trophy.

A broken thermometer in a sealed church envelope.

A mailbox full of driftwood.

Pretentious French Film in Black and White

On a postwar Parisian street
a buzz hums in the background
as a girl throws sheet music
over a high park wall.

The hum is an old woman,
seen through open shutters,
standing in the cold light
of an open refrigerator.

Down on the cobblestones,
lovers sighing in the background,
a bulimic full of Turkish Delight
runs with a balloon, naked,

past a beggar who coughs
silver dust from his hands,
which is swept away by a man
with a broom who calls

like a fishmonger, "You think
me despiséd?" Cut away
and the sighing has moved upstairs,
above the haberdasher, where

on a bed, a thin woman twists
in her lover's arms, her skirt
hitched, her eyes circling
the vortex of his ear. Night

falls. A gypsy lights a lantern,
shadows shift across a window

in a back alley where a woman,
child on hip, says so the neighbors hear,

"I love you, can't you see, Michel?"
A cigarette at his lips, he says
to himself as he walks away,
"I only see despair."

Fishing in the Age of Telos

I used to go with friends, Joel most often,
who had all the good tackle and knew
where the bass bit best. Close at hand,
standing just there, lipping a Camel
and casting, we didn't have to say much.
The biggest was nearly eighteen inches,
caught near a drain, not a pretty place
to spend an afternoon but a great place
to fish—a gravity drawing the silence
closed, filling it full of slight wind
and still slighter slurps of shoes not meant
to ever get wet. He went on his way
home after work most days, just a few
throws sometimes to calm him, then back
to the neighborhood rattle. A wise man,
in ways, Joel, a good friend who helped
me move though it was just us two, who
doesn't show up on a search, though
I've looked. I imagine he's tying a lure
as I type, or better still, setting a hook
near the culvert again. He'd reel it in
and hold it and throw it back. Me, I don't
even own a rod these days, instead I sit
in this cluttered office on the third floor,
wired and with a wind where the window
won't quite close, blowing slightly, nearly
as subtly across this deaf grey screen
as the breeze in this memory of fishing.
Sitting typing, casting lines of lukewarm
prose up and over the horizon into friends'
homes, homes I've never even seen.
I'm like an old New England troller,

dozens of baited lines bobbing in the fog,
their hooks swallowed up on the horizon
somewhere all my friends now gather,
alone, convinced we're all fishing together.

After the Party, I Think of the Serenity Prayer

Natalie said she didn't believe in sin,
and I said apparently. Her friend
with fire-red hair, well, I've thought
a lot about her. How she tucked
her legs up under. Like a director
making a strange choice casting
a movie, they're friends. Joint cohabit-
ation sisterhood something, who knows.
The light pushing at the shadow.

After Natalie ruined the party, we smoked
in the back room. Behind her eyeliner,
she was furious. Too many women
and only one man. Mean women lose.
Birds peck at a carcass in a Western.
We leave her like a fire laid and lit.

Outside, a rope falls from the sky
and we're glad to get away, so her friend
and I climb it. It's just us two dangling
and she says, look! and the hand
of the moon lifts a glass, and we drink,
and meteors shoot from the four corners,
so we ride one home, and then later
in our wool coats eating pasta
from the pot at sunrise, we realize
it's futile, the romance of it, we have
someone better waiting in the future,
and yes, indeed, in hindsight what a good
choice that was.

# FOUR

First Light

To wake alone
and walk alone through
a shadow-long day
often seems easier than

to wake together
and together share
the old long shade
that hangs between

us two. What need
have we for light
except to push against
this ancient absence?

The Word in Edgewise

Love's rusted edges,
all its dents,
the fundraiser sledgehammer car of all words,
weedy in its dings, sits
till we rend its door open
and look inside. And there

on the passenger side
a drunken stubborn angel
motions us with a mighty hand
to drive. And drive we do

till love burns in the traffic hum,
and each car's passing stereo screams
'the pain doesn't matter much
in the end.' We began

by simply asking this:
What makes us huddle here
naked and clutching love so desperately?
We are not shy on evidence.

The tent revival's matted grass says
widespread love's been had here.

The wind as it spills through the vane,
the ground in the clutches of roots,

the bent tree the cold sky
filters through, so long and empty,

asks, as we idle,
'Can we stand the wind
without love or something like it
in this cold and vast Nebraska,
this unkempt, middling place?'

Just drive, you graceless fool,
before the weather breaks.

Dialogue on Architecture and Palmistry

What if my hand's in my pocket

    and my arm's in the keyhole it makes

and you squint in the courtyard of the house I said we
    should fix up

    and I say it's really nice but for the pile of pipes and bricks next
        to the steps.

Eyes closed, you breathe it in and say you can smell the
    snow melting.

    The snow is melting, that's right. But what else?

Our boots have salt stains all up their sides.

    I see. It's like yesterday, when I read the things around us like a
        palm.

Yes, walking the lifeline down Main street, you stopped near
    that house we should buy but you said, actually,

    I liked the picket fence and it could stand a coat of paint then, eyes closed, you breathed it in and said the fence is,

    what's the wrinkle up top near the fingers? The

    fence is that line.

    And when I said that, I took my thumb and held it

like an architect building a lifesize model of the thing he'd

    build if there were time to get it just right.

    Then I blinked but didn't say, until later, drinking coffee at a

        diner,

that when you opened your eyes, you felt your soul come

    back inside

    just like it does after sneezing.

On Diffidence

I cannot distill sunlight into food
or perform the pure union over eight hours
of tantric sex. I have little control
over my heart-rate, cannot move my little toe,
or stand the taste of eggplant. I have tried
and failed to raise the dead.

I ignore all flashbacks. I've not been able to
overcome *one*, my fear of insanity,
two, my fear of driving, *three*, fear of being
alone forever, *four*, of love. Because
of all this, there's an anxious serum
drip of serotonin I can feel some days
leaking down the back of my head.

Some facts are that I don't eat before I drive
long distances because food is a drug;
that I call my friends at all hours
because I can't sleep because
I have thoughts like bad children's stories;
that it recently took me nine dates
to kiss a woman. I cannot feel

ashamed of being only human.
I cannot play any woodwinds,
or play the piano unless I hold down the sustain
for effect. I have never been to Disneyland.
I feel artificial in the suburbs, walking through
the parking lots out near the highway,
ordering Kentucky Fried, extra crispy.

I have gotten over my disdain for my father
who was hard on me and has told me
since I was a child that a man is never a man
until his father dies. I have come
to appreciate my mother
who doesn't read much
because she already knows most things
in books, because she's addicted to people
and living, because she doesn't explain
her lasagna. I cannot understand my sister,
who runs a restaurant, dries basil over the sink
in her kitchen, pets her cats while on the phone.

I have not been able to crack the code
in issues of gender. I once spent three years
trying to not label anyone or anything, thinking
we are all one. I had a hard time
falling in love with a woman at the time
because she didn't exist. I never wanted it to end.
But things do. I cannot
seem to get that through my head.

I admit, I have never been able to do
a good cartwheel, or master the handspring,
could never tuck my head up under.

I have never lifted a hand
to get my point across. Except once,
and I would take that back.
My sister is convinced that regret
is pointless. I cannot take it

back. Ever. I cannot
bring myself to a sublime state

of forgiveness. I do not believe
in grace. I am afraid of distance,
of closeness, of the hand of God.
I believe in personal gravity
and the gravity of places that I used
to live. Like now,

I am sitting at my computer
and there is pressure to my left,
which is where Michigan is,
an old flame is, my parents.
I cannot help feeling that my grandmother,
seventy-seven and in the hospital
with a bad heart, may die.
Please, if you would,

settle me down in my chair.
It's a quarter past three. Time
to take things harder. Either tell me
the things I should work on
or knock me down so I'll finally quit
talking altogether. It's time to

make way, Moses, impart
the lesson, partly embarrassment.
I was twenty-five before I realized
the root of humiliation is a lack
of humility. But I still can't swallow,
this pill is very large and bitter.

Prognosis: Cataract

Why can't we take this sunlight and cold air,
turn it over like sheet music between beats
and look at what's beneath?

It's the curtain between the room
and the window.
When the cataract's removed, vision returns.

Put a poultice of snow and burnt leaves
on the eyes and wait three days
for clarity. The other night

you asked, Would you make me some tea,
and I answered without saying,
walked to the kitchen slowly.

It was snowing outside for the third time that day,
the trees bent low from the weight.
Today, the snow is blown

round my car in a crescent,
a high and mighty form, a comet
in still frame before I shovel it clear.

It's so bright out, stark and frigid,
the sun's a contradiction,
the houses hold tight to the cold.

Yes, I'll get the mail on my way up, I say,
you at the door in your socks,
and I think, for a second, we're dancing,

the two of us, the first time in months,
the snow and mail just larger hands
at our waists, something bigger

than I alone could make. Everyone clears
the snow from their walk and I think,
Would it all be one white thing

if we could see it all at once?

Conception

Sometimes it wells up inside, this itch,
this lingam with a word at its tip,
and God I want to force one thing

in another just to make it something new,
the way sunlight fucks leaves into lemons.
Houses down the block, brooding

and still, line up in a summer staleness.
I'd like to open the thighs of this street,
I think, and see to it. We spread ourselves

so thin these days, I say instead, both
staring at the ceiling in silence. We tire
of trying, so go for a walk. Holding

her hand past houses we might buy,
talking them into homes, dressing up
our thoughts with nightclothes

and underthings, the intimate pleasantry
of dreams. The mind is its own place.
Only in such places is creation ever tired.

Dowry Aubade

Even in hindsight, I'd gladly deny
the thirty-seven cans of snap beans,
two thousand chunks of fool's gold,
a grammar guide for young boys,
and Coney Island love thermometer
your family thought was needed
to persuade the likes of me to marry
the good looking, sexy likes of you.

What would I do, anyway, with
a rolled-up carpet of silver thread,
butterfly collections from the museum,
six white spiraling church steeples
looking out across the valley of pines
just south of the black dirt farmland
seeded with sunflowers and irises?

Could they ever top the way you
kneed the rug with your feet at night,
your reflection in the television
watching old Egyptian movies,
the small sounds of you watering
your flowers on the porch, or how
you hold my chair back when you
read over my shoulder on Sundays?

The answer, quite simply, is no.
What use could I have for such things
when the sunrise comes and you go
to the gym, barely waking me. Know
the first thing I do when I finally wake
is make the bed, and where you were

is the cat and he's not asked anything
but for your return, tolerant of me, but
really wanting the riches you earned.

Anticipating Bob Hicok

I'm keeping This Clumsy Living shelved,
there, out of reach, the want of reading it
like a housewife's looking-forward-to
of the Carlisles' party on Saturday night.

A small yearning, really, but one aware
that Vern will bring his circus fleas,
Sally, her mink stole that growls,
and Sam's young lover of fourteen days

whose scuba fetish is already an issue
will light her Dunhills with a hand lens.
In light of this, I'll wait, and choose
(as monks who eat sole grains of rice),

Pope's Essay on Man or whatnot,
and see myself akin to this housewife,
who, kids napping in silence upstairs,
picks out a dress, the slinky number,

wondering what's better than waiting
for a party? Often not the party.
Truth be told, there's wisdom in waiting.
To appreciate heaven well, it's said,

'tis good to have fifteen minutes of hell.
So watch for a while the just-seeded
lawn's long pause, stare as the plumb bob
slowly swings in search of its vertical,

and wait. Lie low till the time's right,
believe it'll be worth it. At midnight

on the fortieth day of silence open it,
flitting the pages at random at first,

then, in the brief lull between pages
stare out the old back window
to the mercury light humming in the vast
green vacancy of Wind-in-Wood Drive

where our pajamaed children fill the streets
and stand looking on as the moon's sliver
casts down beams like cane poles, baited
with sugared spoonfuls of light

the children eat in silence, heads up
as in prayer, till filled, they fall
into dust, blown like seeds across
the well-watered lawn of heaven.

What May Come of a Simple Statement

It is clear my children understand
something far richer than I do
when they ask what a dungeon is,
and I say it's a jail beneath a castle
where they chain people up, it's dark,
smells bad, with rats running round,
and they don't give you much bread,
if any at all, and then Emily butts in,
saying maybe the rats bring bread
when no one is looking, and a fable
fills the car as a prisoner is dreamt:
A man so humble he is sent below
for lying but is actually just silent
of what he's seen tending his sheep,
and while indeed he saw the king's reeve
kill the farmer's son who refused
to stand aside, this shepherd never said
a word because he only ever speaks
to the sheep when crossing the ford,
and then only in quiet herding songs
and never to other people, and so
in the dungeon his brown beard grows
and no one visits, he has no friends,
but in the night the jailer, drunk down
the hall, is just noisy enough that rats
slip onto his table, steal a bread hunk,
carry it to the shepherd and feed him,
eyes closed in a desperate wonder,
and then nibble the last for themselves.
So this goes on for years, every night,
till the king gets word the shepherd
is touched somehow by God: he grows

fat without eating a crumb, he is light
of spirit in the midst of such squalor,
and the king decrees a miracle, letting
loose the shepherd in a parade of petals,
his irons split by a cross made a chisel,
he's escorted to a hut near the ford
where he used to sing his sheep across
and granted a small flock to tend by day,
and daily loaves of bread and wheels
of cheese brought by the castle baker,
who carries them fresh in her aprons.
It's then by night, so the children say,
he breaks the bread and invites the rats,
who come sit at his table, taking turns
at the head as he feeds them loaves,
laughing carefully so as not to disturb
the reeve's men passing in the night.

For Redemption's Nigh, All Ye Hangers On

The bus is a lit bulb with us in it, all
black folks but me, a daisy in a field of asters.
There's a young tattooed woman with a boy.
The tat's of Saint Anthony amidst a vine
wrapping her forearm. On the phone
the father of her child, she says, don't do
nothing except show up, and he don't
show up to nothing worth a big goddamn,
neither. Her son's head's at Anthony's feet
till a lurch grabs us all over to the left,
and my book falls at the feet of 'Dante,'
his chain says, and he doesn't pick it up,
and why would he? We were separated
at birth, he and I, and we've stopped looking.
We've slid down and away from paradise
one long, ill-wrought day after the other
till we ended here, looking past one another.
A sad state of affairs to believe somehow
the tire swing has no branch overhead,
that the string between the tin cans is cut.
And the only talk in earshot shoots out
the back of a cell phone to a vague horizon.
Dante's alone in his iPod's zone, same
as me, in ways, on retreat in this sci-fi book
I get finally off the floor, bending down.
Holding fast the rail, I stoop, careful
to look willful 'cause I must admit I want
to impress myself deeply into Dante's
calculated nonchalance, enter his world.
He looks past to the three-frame feedback
of row houses clicking by and I'm smitten
away to another reverie, more distant—

the teetering weight of my kids, too young
for words, waiting at home with a waiting
that's not so much a longing as an absence,
lit from above by something like paradise
they are slowly starting to forget.

Bus

Less the leaving than the placing into other hands,
less the other hands than that they're a stranger's.
A spell of diesel, the sun angling between houses.
John, the driver's name is, the only person on.
It's less his first stop than his last moment of silence.
Less the quick goodbye than the quiet taking leave.
A fire truck and pissing dog assure it's not solemn.
"Well," my wife says gently, "that's something new,"
and scrolls through the nine photos she's taken,
posting the best ones to bend our furthest family
in a new orbit. It's a progression, hands-length
to just within sight, then earshot, to strange oversight.
For them it's less a departure than a going-it-alone,
finding yourself elsewhere, trusting someone's at home.

A Small Fight Involving Sheep Cheese

Sometimes it takes a meat hook,
well actually two of them, to keep
my mind open. I am sorry

about the dishes and the butter,
too many cooks and all that,
but, you see, my big concern

is that you'll grow tired of me
before I die. So please, if you would,
feel free to find new and inventive

ways to keep my ears from closing,
my eyes from shutting, my fool mouth
from speaking. Please grab whatever

funnel is closest and pour the world
down my throat and humble me.
It's funny, but even standing next to

a tree, I sometimes feel tall. Perhaps
a cartoon mallet is in order.
What I'm saying to you right now

is that I like it when you are frank.
I got mad about the dishes—you at me
because I told you to put the butter

in the pasta when it was your recipe.
I had never had sheep cheese
and vermicelli before, I did not know.

Please see that more foolish things
have slipped from men's mouths,
like: *I am leaving forever*

and *I never liked you much, anyway,*
come to mind. But I'll save you
those old stories and instead admit

I am clay and malleable, that
things like this throw me
back on the wheel, spinning.

Suburban Beirut Nocturne

Antelias, the name the Greeks gave this city,
meaning Before the Sun, the sunset's rosy fingers
pulling the sea edge surely seemed similar to home
as sailors leaned over gunwales near nightfall
and the quays and docks lined with old men telling
fishing stories to boys too late getting home.

And where Adib wrenches a stripped bolt off
a Beamer used to be a spice seller next door
to a legume shop next to a fat-armed bureaucrat
whose hat tilted when he coughed, smoking.
I've gotten sorely used to it, it's become home
and home, everyone knows, is often a bore.

Antony's coffee shop abuts the sea and sells
cheap sandwiches to plumbers and bank tellers
who bring their wives for the concrete veranda sunsets.
Follow the river up the valley past the bakery
and we're on the fifth floor, halfway up a tower.
From the balcony the long bend to the sea

unfolds in a dense clot of parking and apartments,
though a rocky-soiled banana grove with its house
for farmhands is napping at the foot of the street.
I recall how in an ancient captain's log was written
'Even the fiercest, bluest gods grow tiresome
without enough priests to shill their wares.'

Wise, that, I think dully, nattering to myself.
Though it's dusk and everything's red, I watch
the thin river where men walk between the blocs
and sometimes stop to light a smoke and move on.

Even the slight dingy bubble of sludge and muck
sliding down the river's concrete byway's empty.

Kids with sparklers dance between parked cars.
A light comes on across the street one floor up.
It's a maid in a small room off a kitchen (I see
through her door to the pots and pans hanging).
Today I woke to her shouting out the window,
talking with a maid in the next building over.

It went on for an hour or more, one sometimes
ducking in to do some small thing, their tongue
so foreign I couldn't glean an inkling. But now
she's alone and I'm bored so I steal her. She's
worrying her sheets into place, putting up her hair.
She steps to the window and starts cranking,

the light behind her as the black blind creeps
down the sash until she's gone. What have I done
to you? Against the sun setting and with me
desperate I've taken your shade and hawked it
like a brothel lineup, invited others to watch.
Days later, she still goes about her work alone.

Forest Ridge Farms Nocturne

'Twas eleven hours in the cube today,
and Fran and the kids look cooked when you
get home, rapt in the flash of a high-def
Rembrandt three group in the great room
while you quickly warm your dinner. The vinyl's
falling off the house next door, you say.
She throws a sexy smile the kids can't read.

Eleven trips she made today, she says,
from school to home, to lunch, to home,
to school, to home to change their clothes,
to softball, grocery, softball, home, and last
a walk out to the drive, to meet you all alone,
a kiss because she missed you, and also
'cause she's lonely, so what is she to do?

Tonight, you say, we'll find the good urge,
to close the door with minutes to spare
and while we lie, we'll talk out our days,
the Blankman account, Em's ankle sprain,
sun rays and the warm grass smell. Tell me,
darling, how you pushed the window open
and stood staring, waist-down naked.

How did you know? she asks. It was around
midday. The lonely quiet turned me on,
so I stared out at the vacancy, the vast
empty chainlink silence of it, till I, close-eyed,
crosslegged underneath, shivered myself,
then napped on the made bed an hour.
Work, I think, would fill the void, she says.

It fills the time, but not the space, it makes
the day go quickly by, and that's what's got *me*
scared these days, you say. The girls are asleep,
she says. A humid waft slips in the window.
That cut-grass smell? You smell that? she says,
That's what got me going. I love you, you say.
This love, these thin walls can't contain it.

About the Author

Sean M. Conrey teaches and coordinates the Project Advance program in the English and Textual Studies department at Syracuse University in Syracuse, New York, where he lives most of the year with his wife, Carol Fadda-Conrey, and his two daughters, Emily and Mira. He spends his summers writing in Beirut, Lebanon. A chapbook of his poems, *A Conversation with the Living*, was published by Finishing Line Press in 2009 and his monograph *Coming to Terms with Place*, a theoretical work concerned with how language affects our sense of place, was published in 2007. An album of original songs, *Hosmer and Ninth*, recorded with The Mercury City String Band, a revolving group of musicians, is available on CD and online through Creative Commons. This is his first full-length collection of poetry.

Our Mission

The mission of Brick Road Poetry Press is to publish and promote poetry that entertains, amuses, edifies, and surprises a wide audience of appreciative readers. We are not qualified to judge who deserves to be published, so we concentrate on publishing what we enjoy. Our preference is for poetry geared toward dramatizing the human experience in language rich with sensory image and metaphor, recognizing that poetry can be, at one and the same time, both familiar as the perspiration of daily labor and as outrageous as a carnival sideshow.

Also Available from Brick Road Poetry Press

www.brickroadpoetrypress.com

Dancing on the Rim by Clela Reed

Possible Crocodiles by Barry Marks

Pain Diary by Joseph D. Reich

Otherness by M. Ayodele Heath

Drunken Robins by David Oates

Damnatio Memoriae by Michael Meyerhofer

Lotus Buffet by Rupert Fike

The Melancholy MBA by Richard Donnelly

Two-Star General by Grey Held

Chosen by Toni Thomas

Etch and Blur by Jamie Thomas

Water-Rites by Ann E. Michael

Bad Behavior by Michael Steffen

Tracing the Lines by Susanna Lang

Rising to the Rim by Carol Tyx

Treading Water with God by Veronica Badowski

Rich Man's Son by Ron Self

Just Drive by Robert Cooperman

The Alp at the End of My Street by Gary Leising

About the Prize

The Brick Road Poetry Prize, established in 2010, is awarded annually for the best book-length poetry manuscript. Entries are accepted August 1st through November 1st. The winner receives $1000 and publication. For details on our preferences and the complete submission guidelines, please visit our website at www.brickroadpoetrypress.com.